Heinemann
Research

Life in a Rookery

Penguins

Heinemann
LIBRARY

Richard and Louise Spilsbury

H www.heinemann.co.uk/library

To order:
Phone 44 (0) 1865 888066
Send a fax to 44 (0) 1865 314091
Visit the Heinemann Bookshop at www.heinemann.co.uk/library to browse our catalogue and order online.

First published in Great Britain by Heinemann Library, Halley Court, Jordan Hill, Oxford OX2 8EJ, part of Harcourt Education.
Heinemann is a registered trademark of Harcourt Education Ltd.

Editorial: Nicole Irving and Georga Godwin
Design: Ron Kamen and Celia Floyd
Picture Research: Rebecca Sodergren and Ginny Stroud-Lewis
Production: Viv Hichens

Originated by Dot Gradations Ltd
Printed in China by WKT Company Limited

ISBN 0 431 18266 3 (hardback)
08 07 06 05 04
10 9 8 7 6 5 4 3 2 1

ISBN 0 431 18273 6 (paperback)
09 08 07 06 05
10 9 8 7 6 5 4 3 2 1

British Library Cataloguing in Publication Data

Spilsbury, Richard and Spilsbury, Louise
Animal Groups: Penguins – Life in a Rookery
598.4'7156
A full catalogue record for this book is available from the British Library.

Acknowledgements

The Publishers would like to thank the following for permission to reproduce photographs:

FLPA/Minden Pictures/Tui de Roy p. 18; Guillaume Dargaud pp. 14, 22; National Geographic p. 15; NHPA/Alberto Nardi p. 9; NHPA/Brian Hawkes p. 21; NHPA/David Middleton p. 5 (top); NHPA/Eckart Pott p. 5 (bottom); NHPA/Haroldo Polo p. 24 (bottom); NHPA/J. & A. Scott p. 19; NHPA/Martin Harvey p. 28; NHPA/Rich Kirchner p. 20; NHPA/Rod Planck p. 14; NPL/Doug Allan pp. 10, 11, 13a, 17, 26; NPL/Lynn Stone p. 13b; NPL/Peter Bassett p. 7; Oxford Scientific Films/Ben Osbourne p. 8; Oxford Scientific Films/Daniel Cox p. 24 (top); Oxford Scientific Films/Doug Allan pp. 23, 27; Oxford Scientific Films/Kjell Sandved p. 4; Punchstock p. 25; Still Pictures/Roland Seitre p. 16.

Cover photograph of the group of penguins, reproduced with permission of Corbis/Paul A. Souders.

The Publishers would like to thank Colin Fountain for his assistance in the preparation of this book.

Every effort has been made to contact copyright holders of any material reproduced in this book. Any omissions will be rectified in subsequent printings if notice is given to the Publishers.

Contents

Any words appearing in the text in bold, **like this**, are explained in the Glossary.

What are penguins?

Penguins are birds that live by or in the sea most of their lives. There are seventeen different **species** (kinds) of penguins in the world. Although each species is slightly different, all adult penguins have black backs and white bellies. Like all birds, penguins are animals that have wings, a beak, bodies covered in feathers, and they lay eggs. Unlike most other birds, penguins cannot fly – although it looks as if they are flying when they swim underwater!

Why can't penguins fly?

Penguins' wings are **adapted** for life in water. They have become narrower, stiffer and flatter than other bird wings, and the wing feathers are short, so they are no use for flying. A penguin's wings look more like the flippers of a dolphin, and they help them to move through water just as a dolphin's flippers do.

Emperor penguins, like this one, are the largest species at over a metre tall. The smallest are the Little Blue (or fairy) penguins that can grow up to 41 centimetres.

Do penguins live in groups?

Penguins are some of the most **social** birds in the world. Although penguins spend some time alone, they spend much of their lives with other penguins of the same kind. Penguins form groups to swim and dive, to feed, to travel from one place to another and also to **breed**. The groups of penguins that form at breeding time are called rookeries.

This is a rockhopper penguin. Its colourful head crest makes it look quite different from other species.

Chinstraps are the commonest penguin species. They have white faces and a thin black stripe under their chin. They are on average about 70 centimetres tall.

What is a rookery of penguins like?

A rookery of penguins is made up of lots of families. Each family consists of a **male** and **female** pair of adults and their baby penguins. Most male and female penguins look alike. The baby penguins are smaller and covered in fluffy down feathers. Baby penguins are called **chicks**. Penguins gather in different-sized rookeries. The biggest rookeries number several million penguins, the smallest a few hundred. A rookery almost always contains penguins of only one **species**.

When do rookeries form?

Most penguin species gather together on particular areas of land at particular times of year to **breed**. For example, Adélie and chinstrap penguins come ashore in spring to form their rookeries for a few months. They gather together at this time because it is the best time of year to have and raise young. By the time the young penguins are learning to catch food for themselves, it is summer and there is plenty of food about.

What are rookeries like?

Rookeries are incredibly busy, noisy places. Penguin families squabble loudly over nest sites, chicks cry out for food and parents call to young that have wandered too far. Rookeries also smell. This is because of the huge amount of guano that builds up in the area. People who have visited rookeries say they could smell them long before they could see them!

The largest penguin rookeries in the world can cover as much space as a large town! These are chinstrap penguins in Antarctica.

Do rookeries change?

When the **breeding season** is over for the year, most rookeries split up into smaller groups. These smaller groups may spend the rest of the year together in the ocean. For example, king penguins form groups of between five and twenty penguins that swim and feed together. When it is time to **breed** again all of the smaller groups return to the same place and join up to form large rookeries.

A few **species** of penguin, such as the African penguin, spend their whole lives in rookeries. This is usually because they live in places where it is warmer and young can be born and raised at any time of the year.

Most rookeries, like this rookery of Adélie penguins, break up at the end of the breeding season each year.

Where do penguins live?

All seventeen **species** of penguins live in the **Southern Hemisphere**. Most penguins live on the coasts of Antarctica or on islands nearby. Some live in warmer places on the coast of South America, Africa, Australia and New Zealand. For example, Galapagos penguins live on warm **tropical** islands, closer to the **Equator** than any other penguin. Even if they visit warmer shores, all penguins live near cold ocean **currents** because this is where the **prey** that they need to eat lives.

Most of the world's penguins live on or near the icy shores of Antarctica.

For most of the time, penguins are in the sea. Most species of penguins spend at least two-thirds of their lives in water. When they come ashore, penguins live mainly on islands or quiet coastal places where there are few other animals. This is important because the fact that they cannot fly would make them easy prey for **predators**.

Where do rookeries gather?

Rookeries of different species gather in different kinds of places. Emperor penguins form rookeries on flat areas of solid ice near the coast, which are sheltered from wind. The small gentoo penguins gather on ice-free ground on beaches and cliffs. Chinstrap rookeries settle on rock-covered steep slopes. In warmer places, some kinds of penguins, such as the Little penguin, of Australia, make burrows to have their young in.

Burrowing penguins, like these Humboldt penguins in Peru, make many burrows close by each other.

What is Antarctica like?

Antarctica has the worst weather in the world. It is so extremely cold that ice and snow almost always cover the ground. High winds blast across the lower shores and in winter there are months without daylight. It is a good place for penguins to live because there are large amounts of their favourite foods in the cold waters.

How do penguins get around on land?

On land, penguins grip ice or rock with their clawed and **webbed** feet. When penguins walk on their short strong legs, they waddle – they sway back and forth between steps. They may also hop or toboggan if they need to go faster. Tobogganing is just what it sounds like – penguins lie on their bellies and push themselves along with their wings.

How do they swim in the sea?

Penguins are superbly **adapted** for swimming in water. They have a **streamlined** shape that makes them look like torpedoes. This helps them to shoot through the water fast, with their head tucked back into their neck. Their stiff and paddle-like wings move them along. They use their legs, feet and tail for steering.

Penguins walk slowly. To move fast on ice they toboggan along on their bellies!

How do penguins survive in the cold?

The Antarctic is a tough place to live, but the penguins that live there are well **adapted** for survival. They have different features that stop them from getting too cold.

How do penguins keep warm?

Penguins have a thick layer of fat to keep them warm but their feathers also keep out the cold. Penguins have more feathers than most other birds. Their feathers are also shorter and they grow close together. The top feathers are oily and overlap each other tightly so they form a warm and waterproof coat. Next to their skin they have short, downy (fluffy) feathers that trap a layer of warm air. Their dark back feathers also help to absorb or soak up any warmth that comes from the sun during the daytime.

On land, penguins keep wings tight by their sides and tuck their head in their neck to keep warm when still. In the water, they keep active and busy to stop themselves getting too cold.

Do penguins clean their feathers?

Groups of penguins are often seen cleaning their feathers because the feathers need to be in good condition. They use their beaks to spread oil from a gland near their tail all over their feathers. This oily coating is what makes the feathers waterproof. If their feathers got wet the penguins would get very cold and they could not survive in Antarctica.

When penguins stand on ice, they tip up their feet so they are resting on their heels and wedge-shaped tail. This reduces the amount of skin that touches the ice.

Adult male emperor penguins huddle together to protect themselves from the extreme cold and biting winds while they **incubate** their eggs by keeping them warm between their feet.

Do penguins ever lose their feathers?

Penguins lose their feathers once a year, which gets rid of worn-out feathers so that strong new ones can grow in their place. This is called **moulting**. For about two to four weeks this means a penguin's coat is thin and patchy. During this time, they have to keep out of the water and so cannot feed. They eat lots before moulting so they can live off their fat store.

New feathers grow up from below and push out a penguin's old worn-out feathers when it moults.

How do penguins keep cool in warm places?

Penguins in warmer places have thinner feathers and a thinner fat layer than penguins in Antarctica. If they get too warm they move into a shady spot and pant. They hold their wings out in the breeze to cool them. Some, like the Little penguins of Australia, stay cool at sea during the day. They gather in groups to come ashore in the evening when it is cooler and sleep in burrows underground.

What do penguins eat?

Penguins eat mostly small fish, squid and crabs. They catch and swallow their food whole while they are swimming. Some **species** of penguins prefer particular types of food. For example, Adélie penguins eat mostly krill (small shrimp-like animals) – they can swallow up to 1 kilogram each day!

How far do penguins go to find food?

Different species travel different distances to find food. Some groups of penguins, such as Adélie penguins, feed together in shallow waters quite near to the coast. Others, such as emperor penguins, travel much further away, to look for **prey** in deep waters. In fact, king and emperor penguins may **migrate** over 620 miles (1000 kilometres) to find large fish and squid.

Some penguins may be away from land feeding for about ten hours at a time, while others may be at sea for days or weeks.

How do penguins catch their food?

Penguins feed mostly during the day. They catch prey by seeing it and swimming after it quickly. They have good eyesight and they can see better underwater than they can on land, where they seem to be a bit short-sighted! Scientists think that some penguins manage to catch certain types of fish and squid at night because these animals glow in the dark.

Most penguins have a sharp beak that is short and thick and has a strong grip. They also have mouths and tongues lined with little backward-pointing spines to help them hold on to slippery prey. Some, like the emperor and king penguins, have beaks that curve downwards. This helps them catch fast-moving fish and squid in deep waters.

Penguins catch food using their beak. This Adélie penguin's beak has sharp edges to grip fish. The spikes on the inside stop their prey escaping.

What do penguins drink?

All animals need to drink water to survive. To get water, penguins eat snow and drink fresh water and sea water. Too much salt from sea water could harm their bodies so they get rid of it from a special **gland** in their beak.

Emperor penguins dive for around two to eight minutes. Most dives are within 21 metres of the surface.

How deep can penguins dive?

Most of the prey that penguins eat swims near the surface of the oceans, so they do not have to dive deeply to catch it. Penguins cannot breathe underwater so they hold their breath for a few minutes while they dive. They usually dive down 20 to 40 metres. Different species dive and swim at different speeds, but most can swim at about 9 miles (14 kilometres) per hour – that is over twice the speed of the fastest human swimmer!

Do penguins hunt in groups?

Many penguins hunt for food on their own, although close to other penguins from their group, but some kinds of penguins actually work together to catch prey.

Groups of Humboldt penguins hunt for **shoals** of fish such as anchovies and pilchards. When they spot a shoal, the members of the team bob their heads to give the signal to dive together. They dive towards the fish from all sides at once, which forces the shoal to form a tight ball. This makes it easy for the penguins to swim straight into the ball to feed. People have also seen emperor penguins working together in this way.

These Galapagos penguins are working as a team to have a better chance of catching plenty of fish in the sea around the Galapagos Islands.

How do penguins communicate?

Animals in a group **communicate** – pass information to each other – about different things. They may communicate to threaten another penguin or a **predator**, attract a mate (partner to **breed** with) or find their young. Penguins communicate by sound and **displays**.

What sounds do penguins make?

Different **species** of penguins make different kinds of calls. For example, Humboldt penguins make a braying sound like donkeys, chinstraps screech loudly and king penguins make a trumpeting noise. Individual penguins all sound slightly different too. This is important for partners to find each other and their **chicks** among hundreds of others in a large rookery. Many penguin groups use a special call at sea to keep in touch with each other. Sound travels well across and in water and one king penguin can hear another calling from over half a mile (over 1 kilometre) away!

Penguins have excellent hearing and communicate a lot by sound. They hear sounds through small holes just behind their eyes.

What displays do penguins use?

Penguins also use displays to show how they feel. A display is when an animal does certain things or moves in certain ways to communicate with others. Penguins use several different kinds of displays. For example, they display one way to show that a particular nest area belongs to them and in another way to frighten off an intruder. A **male** penguin also uses special displays to tell a **female** he wants to breed with her. He may do a lot of head bowing, or wave his wings about. He may also stand up straight with his wings held as far back as he can reach and make a loud wailing sound.

Male Adélie penguins often bring females a gift of a stone. Stones are valuable to these penguins because they use them to build nests. Males give these presents to show they would make a good partner.

Adult penguins usually return to the rookery site they were born in to **breed**. That is why rookeries become so large. Most **females** pair up with the same **males** every year. Young adult penguins have to find a new partner.

What are penguin nests like?

Most penguins make their nests out of piles of grass, moss, mud, stones or feathers on the ground. Some penguins make nests in burrows. Humboldt penguins make burrows in deep piles of their own **guano** (droppings). The female of most **species** of penguins usually lays two eggs. Exceptions are emperor and king penguins, which lay only one. Different species lay eggs of different sizes and shapes. They may be white, blue or green. Most penguin parents take turns to **incubate** the eggs. While one sits on the nest, the other goes to sea to feed.

Gentoo penguins make their nests out of all sorts of things, from pebbles to **moulted** feathers. Some, like this pair, make their nests out of plants and twigs.

Why do penguins breed in rookeries?

Have you heard the expression 'There is safety in numbers'? Penguins breed in rookeries for that reason – to protect and defend their young. In a rookery the penguins lay their eggs at roughly the same time so all the **chicks** are about the same age. The many chicks huddle in groups for safety, guarded from **predators** by a few adults, while parents are away at sea finding them food.

Male emperor penguins incubate their eggs by holding them close to their bodies, off the ice on top of their feet.

Do all penguins make nests?

Emperor and king penguins do not make nests. The males carry a single egg in a flap of skin on their feet. They gather in groups and incubate the eggs for two months while the females are away feeding. They lose almost half their body weight because they use their body fat as food. When the female returns, it is their turn to feed.

What do chicks eat?

At first, parents take it in turns to fetch food for the chicks. They carry fish back in part of their stomach and then regurgitate it (bring it up) to feed the youngsters. As chicks get bigger, both parents have to go to sea at the same time to get enough food for them.

When do chicks become adults?

Penguin chicks stay with their parents until they have grown a waterproof set of feathers. This takes over a year for king penguins, but for most species it takes less than ten weeks. With waterproof feathers, the young penguins can go to sea to fetch their own food. Some species of penguin are ready to have young of their own when they are about three years old; other species do not begin to breed until they are eight years old.

Young penguins usually peck at their parent's beak and cry out to get their parents to regurgitate food for them.

When both parents are away fetching food, older penguin chicks huddle together in groups to keep warm and safe. Often, one or two adults stay behind to guard the group from predators.

These young chinstrap penguins are moulting their downy baby feathers ready to grow an adult set. Once they have their adult feathers, it is time for the penguins to take care of themselves.

Do penguins fight?

When animals live in groups there are often arguments. **Males** in a rookery squabble over finding a **female**. Females and males argue over nest sites and the materials needed to build a nest.

In any disagreement, penguins try to avoid a fight, using **displays** to warn off an enemy. They might stare at their opponent, or approach them walking in a zig-zag way. Some use beak slapping – they shake heads and slap beaks together. If these displays don't work, the penguins fight. Penguins fight beak to beak, by lunging towards each other and pecking or biting. In a large rookery, the space between nests is usually as far as a penguin can peck out to keep others away while still sitting on its eggs!

These penguins are fighting by slapping their beaks against each other. A penguin's beak is sharp and strong and can cause quite a lot of damage.

What dangers do penguins face?

Penguins face many dangers. While they are at sea, many ocean **predators** try to catch and eat penguins. These include leopard seals, sea lions, sharks and orcas (killer whales). On land, penguins have few predators, although sea lions sometimes follow them on to land to try to catch them. Rats, dogs, cats, snakes, foxes and birds, such as skuas, eat eggs and **chicks** if they are left alone by their parents, but these animals would never be able to catch healthy adult penguins.

Leopard seals are one of the penguin's worst enemies.

Why are penguins black and white?

Penguins have black backs and white bellies to help them escape predators when they are in the water. Animals swimming above them find it hard to spot penguins' black backs against the dark waters of deep oceans. Their white bellies make them hard to spot from below, as a predator looks up towards the light sky. This is called counter-shading.

How do penguins escape from predators?

Penguins sometimes escape predators by pecking out at them, swimming fast or leaping out of the water and out of reach or onto land. Penguins also call out warnings to others in their group to give them the chance to get away as well.

What else harms penguins?

Many penguins die at sea, usually from starvation. This may be caused by a lack of fish in a particular area, or because bad weather and rough water makes it difficult to catch any. If adults die at sea in the **breeding season**, eggs and chicks back at the rookery will die, because they have no one to look after them. Many young penguins die before their first birthday because they have not had enough practice catching fish.

Penguins, like these emperor penguins, can leap almost 2 metres from the water to the safety of a rock or iceberg.

Do people harm penguins?

The biggest danger that penguins face is people. Fishing boats catch so many fish that they make it hard for some penguins to find food. People also cause terrible **pollution** in the oceans. Oil dumped or spilled from ships can harm penguins and their nests. Floating rubbish can tangle or choke them. In some places, people collect penguin **guano** to use as **fertilizer**. Often, they do not leave enough for the penguins that use guano for their nests, so those penguins do not lay eggs.

Oil can ruin a penguin's feathers, leaving them to freeze to death. These conservation workers are cleaning some oiled penguins they rescued.

Who protects penguins?

In the past there were 32 more **species** of penguin than there are today. These birds, such as the great auk, became **extinct** because of people. Today, only a few penguin species, such as the Galapagos, are **endangered**. **Conservation** groups are working to protect these penguins so that we do not lose them as well.

Penguin facts

How do penguins sleep?

Most penguins sleep for a few minutes at a time throughout the day, though they sleep longer at night. At sea they nap sitting in the water; on land they sleep sitting, standing or lying down. Some sleep with their beak tucked under a wing.

What is a waddle of penguins?

Some people call a group of penguins a waddle of penguins, because of the way they walk.

How long do penguins live?

Healthy penguins can live for up to fifteen years. Larger species of penguin generally live for longer – emperor penguins live for twenty years, while rockhoppers live for only ten.

This map shows where different kinds of penguins live in the world.

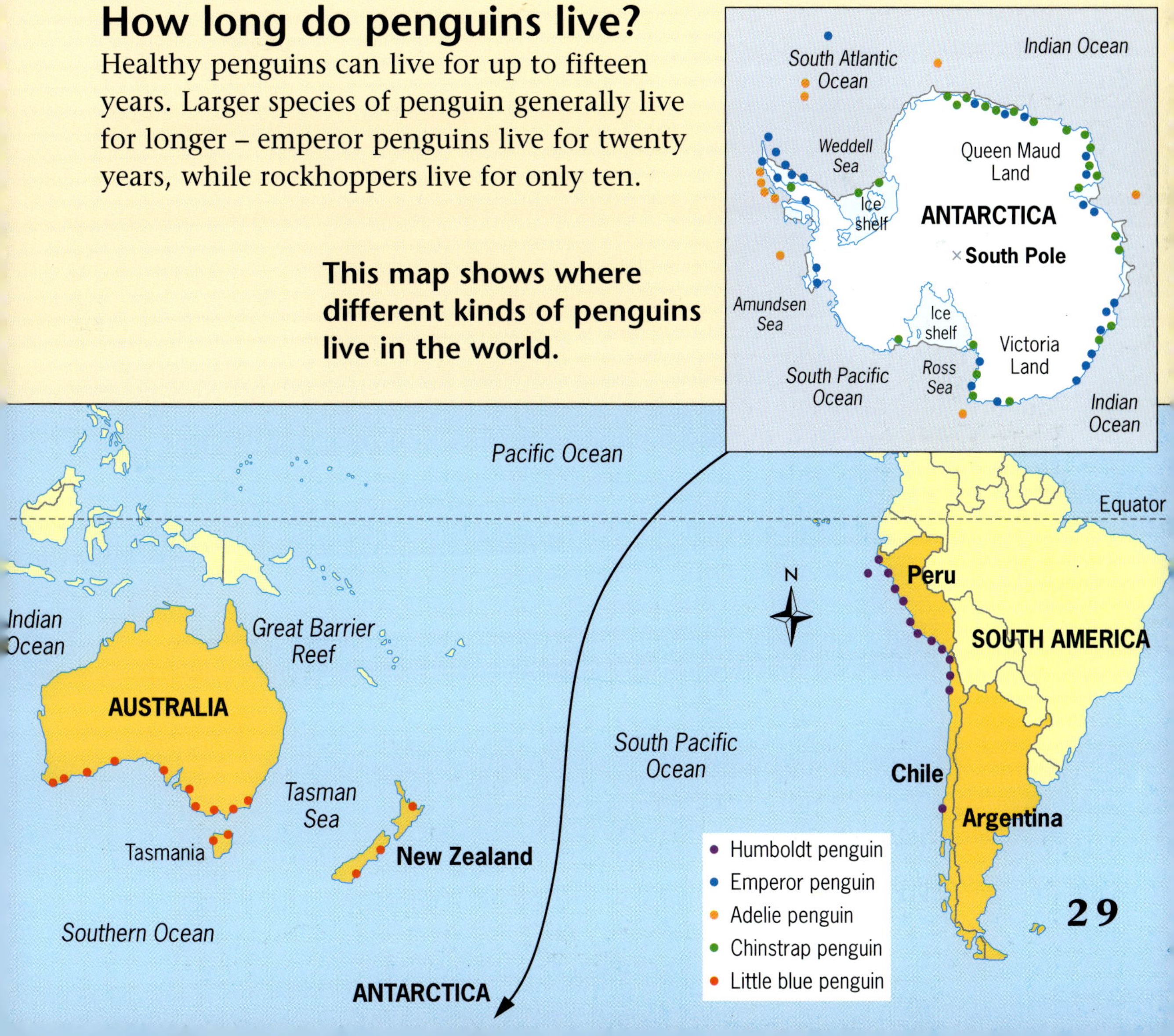

Glossary

adapted describes special features that a species of living things has developed over millions of years to survive in their particular habitat
breed when animals mate and have babies
breeding season time of the year when a particular type of animal breeds
chick young bird
communicate pass on a message containing information to another animal or person
conservation taking action to protect living things and places where they live
counter-shading form of camouflage in which the animal is a dark colour on top and a lighter colour underneath
current stream of water moving through surrounding still water
display put on a show of actions that communicates information
endangered when a plant or animal is in danger of becoming extinct
Equator imaginary line around the centre of the Earth. (It is shown on the map.)
extinct when a species has died out and no longer exists
female animal that, when fully grown, can become a mother. A female human is called a woman or a girl.
fertilizer something that farmers put on plants to help them grow faster, bigger or better
glands parts inside an animal's body that make some of the special chemicals and oils it needs
guano bird droppings
incubate keep eggs warm so that the baby inside can grow
male animal that, when fully grown, can become a father. A male human is called a man or boy.
migrate move to a different place to feed and live for part of the year
moult when an animal loses its old feathers and grows new ones
pant breathe with short quick breaths
pollution when part of the natural world is harmed or poisoned
predator animal that hunts, catches and eats other animals (the prey)
prey animal that is hunted and eaten by another animal (the predator)
shoals groups of fish
social living in well-organized groups that work together
Southern Hemisphere half of the Earth that is south of the Equator
species group of living things that are similar in many ways. Male and female animals of the same species can breed to produce healthy young (babies).
streamlined smooth shape that moves through water easily
tropical describes areas around the Equator, which have the hottest weather in the world
webbed describes feet of certain animals, such as ducks and penguins, which have skin between their toes

Find out more

Books

Animals in Order: Penguins: From Emperors to Macaronis, Erin Pembrey Swan (Franklin Watts, 2003)

Our Wild World: Penguins, Cherie Winner (Northword Books, 2002)

Really Wild: Penguins, Claire Robinson (Heinemann Library, 1998)

Websites

Look for penguins in the animal resources' section of the Seaworld site: www.seaworld.org

The website www.nationalgeographic.com has a 'creature feature' with pictures and sounds all about emperor penguins.

At www.bbc.co.uk there are information pages about individual species of penguins in the 'wildfacts' section.

www.enchantedlearning.com has information about penguins and a picture of a penguin you can print out and colour.

Index